ROTTWEILER

BY CORINNE FICKETT

TABLE OF CONTENTS

A Crabtree Seedlings Book

Crabtree Publishing

crabtreebooks.com

School-to-Home Support for Caregivers and Teachers

This book helps children grow by letting them practice reading. Here are a few guiding questions to help the reader with building his or her comprehension skills. Possible answers appear here in red.

Before Reading:

• What do I think this book is about?
  • *I think this book is about Rottweilers.*
  • *I think this book is about bully breeds.*

• What do I want to learn about this topic?
  • *I want to learn about ways to care for a Rottweiler.*
  • *I want to know why a Rottweiler is a bully breed.*

During Reading:

• I wonder why...
  • *I wonder why Rottweilers need to be socialized.*
  • *I wonder why a Rottweiler needs a firm and confident trainer.*

• What have I learned so far?
  • *I have learned that Rottweilers have muscular bodies.*
  • *I have learned that most Rottweilers are black with tan markings.*

After Reading:

• What details did I learn about this topic?
  • *I have learned that Rottweilers are very protective.*
  • *I have learned that bully breeds come from Molosser dogs.*

• Read the book again and look for the vocabulary words.
  • *I see the word breed on page 3 and the word broad on page 7. The other glossary words are found on pages 22 and 23.*

The Rottweiler is a bully **breed**.

Tosa Inu

All bully breeds come from Molosser dogs. These dogs were large and **muscular**.

ALBANIA

NORTH MACEDONIA

BULGARIA

GREECE

TURKE

Athens

FUN FACT

Molosser dogs came from Greece.

Like other bully breeds, Rottweilers have muscular bodies.

Rottweilers also have **broad** chests.

A Rottweiler's coat is short, dense, and a little rough.

Most are black with tan markings.

Most Rottweilers weigh 80 to 135 pounds (36 to 61 kilograms). They stand 22 to 27 inches (55 to 68 centimeters) tall.

 **FUN FACT**

A Rottweiler's average life span is 9 to 10 years.

Rottweilers need to be **socialized**. Socialized Rottweilers are good with kids and other dogs.

Rottweilers are very **protective**. They need a firm and confident trainer.

 **FUN FACT**

Rottweilers have close bonds with their families.

Singer Bruno Mars owns a
Rottweiler named Geronimo.

Rottweilers are great at herding **livestock**.

A Rottweiler can be a wonderful addition to the right family.

Am I Ready to Adopt a Dog?

Adopting a dog is a big responsibility. It is important for you and your family to be fully prepared and committed to providing the best possible care for your furry friend. Take this quiz to see if you and your family are ready to talk about getting a dog.

1. Do you know that dogs require a lot of attention and care?   Yes / No

2. Are you willing to spend time playing, walking, and interacting with a dog every day? Yes / No

3. Do you understand that dogs need regular feeding, grooming, and visits to the veterinarian? Yes / No

4. Are you patient enough to train a dog and teach them basic commands like sit, stay, and come?   Yes / No

5. Is your household free of dog allergies?   Yes / No

6. Do you have enough space in your home and an area for a dog to move around and play? Yes / No

7. Can you commit to caring for a dog for its entire life span?   Yes / No

8. Are you prepared to clean up after the dog, including picking up its poop? Yes / No

9. Can you handle the financial responsibility of providing food, toys, medical care, and other necessities for the dog?   Yes / No

10. Do you understand that dogs need regular socialization with other dogs and people to stay happy and well-behaved?   Yes / No

11. Are you willing to commit to taking care of a dog during busy times or vacations? Yes / No

12. Can you handle the challenges of training and caring for a dog, even when things get tough?   Yes / No

Determine your score by adding up all the "yes" answers.

10-12 Yes answers: You are ready to begin a conversation about adopting a dog.

6-9 Yes answers: You might be ready to think about adopting a dog.

0-5 Yes answers: You are not ready to take on the huge responsibility of adopting a furry friend.

Myths About Bully Breeds

Myth 1

Bully breeds are the most dangerous types of dogs.

Studies have not found that bully breeds are more dangerous than other types of dogs. The American Veterinary Medical Association (AVMA) states that any dog can bite. A dog's individual history and situation determines how likely it is to bite.

Myth 2

Bully breeds can lock their jaws.

No dog breed is able to "lock" its jaws. Usually, larger dogs have stronger bites than smaller dogs.

Myth 3

Bully breeds are more aggressive than other dogs.

Any dog can show aggression. Research shows that aggression is not breed specific. A dog's behavior usually comes from how it is brought up, cared for, and trained.

Myth 4

Bully breeds are cute.

Bully breeds are not just cute—they are adorable! They bring joy to their families.

Glossary

breed (breed): A group of animals, within a species, that share specific physical characteristics

broad (brawd): Wide from side to side

livestock (LAHYV-stok): Animals that are raised on farms for different purposes, such as cows, pigs, sheep, and chickens

muscular (MUHS-kyuh-ler): Having strong, well-developed muscles. Muscles are body parts that help a person or animal move.

protective (pruh-TEK-tiv): Able or showing a strong wish to keep others safe from danger

socialized (soh-SHUH-lahyz): Taught to be comfortable and friendly around others

Index

About the Author

Corinne Fickett lives in Taos, New Mexico with her husband and seven rescue dogs. She enjoys hiking in the desert and painting watercolor landscapes. Her favorite dessert is vanilla ice cream topped with chocolate syrup and rainbow sprinkles.

Written by: Corinne Fickett
Designed by: Kathy Walsh
Series Development: James Earley
Proofreader: Janine Deschenes
Educational Consultant: Marie Lemke M.Ed.

Photographs: All images from Shutterstock.

Crabtree Publishing

crabtreebooks.com   800-387-7650

Copyright © 2025 Crabtree Publishing

All rights reserved. No part of this publication may be reproduced, stored in a retrieval system or be transmitted in any form or by any means, electronic, mechanical, photocopying, recording, or otherwise, without the prior written permission of Crabtree Publishing. In Canada: We acknowledge the financial support of the Government of Canada through the Canada Book Fund for our publishing activities.

Printed in the USA/062024/CG20240201

Published in Canada
Crabtree Publishing
616 Welland Avenue
St. Catharines, Ontario
L2M 5V6

Published in the United States
Crabtree Publishing
347 Fifth Avenue
Suite 1402-145
New York, New York, 10016

Library and Archives Canada Cataloguing in Publication
Available at Library and Archives Canada

Library of Congress Cataloging-in-Publication Data
Available at the Library of Congress

Hardcover: 978-1-0398-4470-4
Paperback: 978-1-0398-4551-0
Ebook (pdf): 978-1-0398-4624-1
Epub: 978-1-0398-4694-4
Read-Along: 978-1-0398-4764-4
Audio: 978-1-0398-4834-4